Flutter-Fly Pendants

These beautiful butterflies are an easy variation of the flower. Add color and elegance to the pendant by adding beads to the lower wings.

SIZE: 2½" x 3"

MATERIALS:
Silver non-tarnish wire (18 gauge, 26 gauge) • 40 Purple seed beads • 1 Clear Silver foiled 10mm rectangle bead • 1 Black/white flower round pressed 10mm glass bead • 24" Purple organza ribbon ¾" wide • 24" Purple silk cord • Crimp ends • Lobster Claw clasp • 2 medium jump rings

INSTRUCTIONS:
Pendant: Make butterflies just like flowers shown on page 7, but separate the wire petals differently to form wings. Group 2-3 petals on each side to be the bottom wings, gently pulling them down. Separate and fan out 3 petals for the top wings. Using 12" of 26 gauge wire for wings, wrap each bottom wing in a diagonal pattern, trim extra wire. Tuck wire ends in existing butterfly wires. Add large bead to center of butterfly by threading a bead onto 26 gauge wire and wrapping around the butterfly center. Trim excess wire and tuck in end.

Beaded wings: Turn a loop in one end of 26 gauge wire to insure beads don't fall off when beading. Pick up beads with wire. Close end with another loop before wrapping wings.

Purple necklace: Use slightly different lengths of ribbon and cording to allow for a wavy ribbon look while wearing. Fold organza ribbon and silk cording in half and attach to pendant with a Lark's Head knot. Add crimp ends to ribbon and cording. Add 6 medium jump rings to one end and a lobster claw clasp to the other end.

**Actual Size
Wire Diagram**

Wrap wire around fingers, leave a 2" tail on each end. Hold looped ends and twist in the opposite direction. Wrap wire ends around the center to secure.

Hook Clasps

Tight Hook

Using 2"-3" of 18 gauge wire, turn loop in one end to connect to necklace/bracelet. Bend length in half over round-nose plier barrel. Add decorative loop to end.

Swirl Hook

Using 2"-3" of 18 gauge wire, turn loop in one end to connect to necklace/bracelet. Turn loop in other end and swirl loosely.

Flat Hook

Using 2"-3" of 18 gauge wire, turn loop in one end to connect to necklace/bracelet. Bend length in half over a medium dowel. Add decorative loop to end.

1. Make an oval loop in one end.

2. Hold oval with pliers; wrap excess wire around neck.

3. Trim excess wire with cutters.

Wire Techniques

To Make the Loop

Hold end of wire with round-nose pliers. Make turn clockwise until end meets main wire, forming a small circle. Make sure end is flush with wire. Flatten loop smoothly with flat-nose or nylon pliers if needed. Loops are the connectors and closers in most bead and wire projects. When learning loop making, use the largest part of the round-nose barrel to turn loop. Once mastered, use the smaller parts of the round-nose barrel to get smaller loops as needed.

1. Bend wire at a 90° angle.

2. Hold end of wire with pliers and bend opposite way.

3. Use pliers to meet wire.

Hook and Eye Closures

Use the combination of hook and eye closure or use the pieces individually as needed.

To Make the Eye

To make an eye, bend an oval loop into end of wire using about 3" of wire. Bend over large mandrel or dowel. Hold with flat-nose pliers and wrap end.

To Make the Hook

Fold the wire in half. • Hold wire with flat-nose pliers. Wrap 1 strand around the other. • Shape the curve. • Bend back the end of the loop. • Slide the hook into the eye for closure.

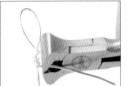

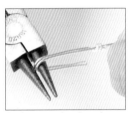

1. Bend 2" or 3" of the wire in half to double.

2. Wrap end with one of the wires.

3. Shape the hook curve.

4. Bend back the end of loop.

5. Slide the hook into the eye for closure.

Wrap Bead Units

Note: Wrapped bead units are stronger than loop bead units.

Use round-nose pliers to bend a right angle into wire length, using 1½" of wire to complete loop and wrap. Roll wire over pliers into a loop, while holding loop in flat-nose pliers tightly, closely wrap short end around long end 3-4 times. Trim excess with wire cutters. Load beads onto long wire. Repeat bead wrap steps at open end to complete wrap bead unit, making sure to leave space beyond last bead for wrapping wire. Trim wire. Each wrap bead unit used 3"-4" of wire depending on loaded bead size.

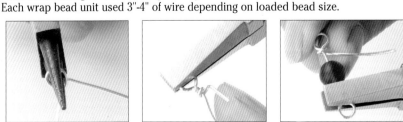

1. Using 3" to 4" of wire bend right angle 1½" from end.

2. Turn angle into a loop with round-nose pliers.

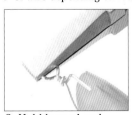

3. Hold looped end tightly. Wrap wire closely around base wire.

4. Add beads and repeat.

Jump Ring Jewelry

Make beautiful jewelry quickly and easily with jump rings. This technique partners beautifully with tube beads, sequins, shells and donut beads. Use crystals, faceted, matte, natural and wood beads to create different looks... from earthy to elegant.

GENERAL MATERIALS:
Silver non-tarnish 18 gauge wire • Beads • Toggle Clasp

BASIC INSTRUCTIONS:
Make large Silver jump rings using wire worker system or large dowel following instructions. Add a bead to each jump ring. Link jump rings together, one after another, joining as many jump rings as needed to make desired chain length.

Bracelet: 20-22 large jump rings
Choker: 45-55 large jump rings
Mid Length Necklace: 60-75 large jump rings

Blue Ice Bracelet

Very delicate and understated, the Blue Ice bracelet has a feminine appeal that will enhance your favorite silk blouse or complement your favorite blue jeans.

SIZE: 8"

MATERIALS:
20 gauge Silver wire jump rings (39 medium, 1 small) • 21 Blue 4mm faceted glass beads • 12mm Lobster Claw clasp

INSTRUCTIONS:
Units: Make 21 loop bead units with Blue faceted beads. See page 6. • Make 39 medium jump rings with 20 gauge Silver wire.
Strand One Formation: 3 jump rings, 2 loop bead units side by side • 3 jump rings, 2 loop bead units side by side • Repeat 4 more times.
Strand Two Formation: 3 jump rings • 1 loop bead unit, 1 jump ring • 1 loop bead unit, 1 jump ring • Repeat 7 more times • add 3 jump rings.
Bracelet: Link together both ends of strands with double jump rings. Attach lobster claw clasp to bracelet with small jump ring. Adjust size by adding or removing jump rings at each end as needed.

Making Jump Rings:

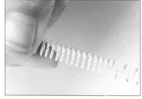

Making Jump Rings: Use 18 or 20 gauge wire, no matter the size. • Twist wire on wire worker or wrap on dowel tightly to form close coil. Slide coil off dowel. Trim jagged ends flush with coil. • Pull coil slightly apart and cut each loop with wire cutters.

1. Coil the wire around dowel.

2. Pull wire apart to separate.

3. Use wire cutters to cut jump rings apart.

4. Use round-nose or flat pliers to open and close by sliding to side.

Aqua Elegance Bracelet

Sparkling sky and water tones in a perfect silver setting bedazzle the eye, making the Aqua Elegance bracelet irresistible.

SIZE: 8"

MATERIALS:
20-22 large jump rings • 2 medium jump rings • 20-22 Aqua faceted 4 x 6mm tube beads • Toggle clasp

INSTRUCTIONS:
Load jump ring with bead and link 20-22 jump rings to form bracelet. Add 1 medium jump ring to each end, adding toggle clasp before closing jump ring.

Loop Bead Units

Use round-nose pliers to turn a loop in one end of the wire. Thread beads onto the wire and turn another loop to complete loop bead unit. Generally each bead unit uses 1" - 2" of wire depending on bead size. Adjust loops to line up at both ends by twisting slightly if needed.

1. Using 1" to 2" of wire, turn loop into end of wire.

2. Add beads.

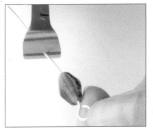

3. Trim wire 1/2" from bead.

4. Close loop bead unit with another loop.

Butterflies and Flowers
Daisy Chain Choker and Earrings

Perfectly elegant for evening wear, this daisy set will also add sparkle to your daily casual attire.

SIZE: 19" choker, 1¾" earrings

MATERIALS:
Silver non-tarnish wire (22 gauge, 20 gauge) • 4 small jump rings • 18 loop bead units • 2 coil beads • 12 Black faceted 8mm beads • 6 Silver flower spacer beads • 24" Black suede cord • Silver flower toggle clasp • 2 crimp ends

INSTRUCTIONS:
Wire flowers: Make 7 small flowers using 24" of 22 gauge Silver wire for each flower. Set 2 aside for earrings. Using 2 smallest fingers, wrap wire around 5-6 times leaving a 1" and a 2" tail at ends before and after wrapping. Remove from fingers, being careful to keep loops together. Continue as directed in Basic Flower Instructions on page 5. After wrapping the center of flower, leave enough wire tail to make a small loop and wrap like the end of a bead wrap. You will need this loop to dangle bead strands from each flower. Join flowers together with a small jump ring making sure flowers are lined up in the same direction.

Loop bead units:
1. Make 14 Black bead units and 8 Silver flower bead units. Set 2 each aside for earrings. Hook together to form dangle strands in this order: Black, flower • Black, Black, flower • Black, flower, Black, flower • Black, Black, flower • Black, flower. Add dangle strands to flower loops with a small jump ring in same order as assembled.
2. Add remaining Black bead units with a small jump ring to flower connector links.

To complete choker: Cut 2 pieces of 12" Black suede cord (1 for each side of choker). Thread one piece of suede cord through second flower petal on one side, fold in half, load Silver coil bead, sliding down to tightly hold suede cord in place. Repeat on other side. Add crimp ends to both sides of the choker. Add toggle clasp.

Earrings: Using flowers set aside, add earring wire to top loop with a small jump ring. Hook Black bead unit and Silver flower bead unit together to form two dangle strands. Add dangle strand to flower bottom loop with a small jump ring.

Wiring Flowers and Butterflies

1. Wrap wire around your fingers leaving a 2" tail on each end.

2. Holding looped ends, twist in the opposite direction twice.

3. Wrap wire ends around the center in opposite directions.

4. Form a loop for hanging with remaining ends.

5. Fan out loops.

6. Attach a bead with another wire.

Fancy Flowers

Remember making flowers at summer camp from tissue paper and pipe cleaners? These fanciful wire flowers will take you right back to your youth with a versatile, easy technique.

BASIC FLOWER MAKING

The length and gauge of wire used depends upon the flower size. The largest flower requires about 2 yards of 18 gauge wire. The smallest flower uses about 24" of 22 gauge wire. The smaller the flower, the thinner the wire needs to be for flexibility. A medium flower uses 1 yard of 20 gauge wire. This is just a guide.

INSTRUCTIONS:

Take length of wire and wrap it around your fingers, or in the case of the largest flower use the palm of your hand, making sure to leave a 1" - 2" tail on both ends before and after wrapping. Wrap 5-6 times to form a nice flower. Remove wire from fingers or hand, keeping wire loops together. Holding looped ends in each hand, twist in the opposite direction, twice in the middle to form a bow tie. Wrap loose wire ends around the center, taking one wire in one direction and the other in the opposite. Form a loop for hanging at the end. Separate wire loops on each side to form flower petals, fanning them out like a deck of cards.

Beauty Pendant

Gorgeous beads give these pendants pizzazz. Midnight Beauty is sure to draw attention at any time of day.

SIZE: 18"

MATERIALS:

Silver non-tarnish wire (24 gauge, 18 gauge) • 4 large jump rings • 1 bead wrap • 2 Jet Black/Aqua Oval 12mm beads • 1 Black faceted 6mm bead • 2 Silver spacer beads • 16" Black velvet ribbon

INSTRUCTIONS:

Flower: Make a large flower with 2 yards of 18 gauge wire. Using the palm of your hand, wrap wire around 6-7 times leaving a 2" - 3" tail at both ends before and after wrapping. Remove from hand, keeping loops together. Continue following Basic Flower Instructions.

Pendant: Use remaining length of wire tail to form a large loop at top of flower. Wrap end around loop base to secure in place. Trim excess.
• Using 12" of 24 gauge Silver wire, attach bead to center of flower, wrapping tightly and going through bead hole twice. Trim excess wire.

Bead Wrap Connector: Make bead wrap unit with beads and spacers to complement flower center. Link flower and bead unit together with 2 large jump rings. Add 2 more jump rings to the remaining end of bead unit to attach pendant to necklace.

Necklace: Add crimp ends and hook ends to Black velvet. String velvet through pendant.

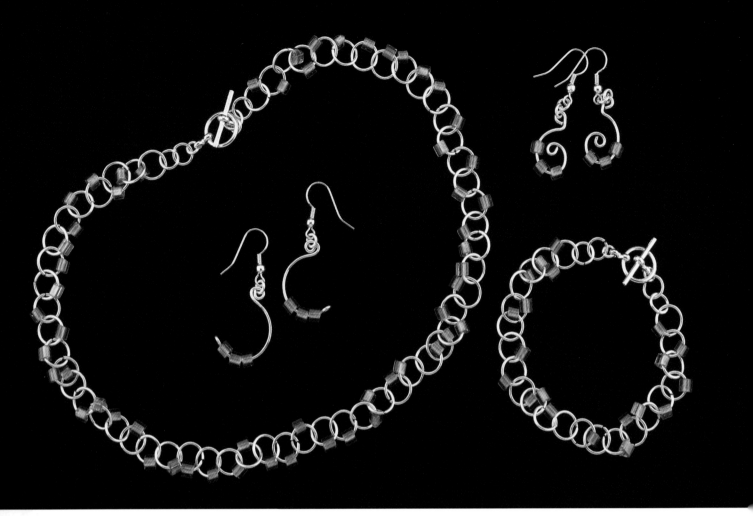

Necklace and Bracelet

1. Make jump rings.

2. Add a bead to each.

3. Link the jump rings together.

'Green with Envy' Jewelry

Capture the look of jade without the weight in this coordinated ensemble.

SIZE: 19" necklace, 8" bracelet, 1" earrings

MATERIALS:
Jump rings (For bracelet: 20-22 large, 4 medium; For choker: 45-55 large, 4 medium; For earrings: 2 extra large, 2 small)
• 71-84 Green Lined Yellow triangle beads
• 2 Toggle clasps • Half hoops • 4 earring wires

INSTRUCTIONS:

Bracelet: Load jump rings with bead and link 20-22 jump rings to form bracelet. Add 2 medium jump rings to each end, adding toggle clasp before closing jump ring.

Choker: Load jump rings with bead and link 45-55 jump rings for choker. Add 2 medium jump rings to each end, adding toggle clasp before closing jump ring.

Earrings: Make extra large jump rings around a round bead tube or thread spool. Make loop in one end to secure beads. Add beads. Turn loop in other end of wire. Attach earring wire to earring with small jump ring.

Loop Earrings

1. Make a tiny loop in one end of the wire.

2. Add beads.

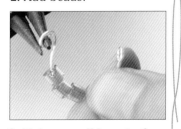

3. Make a small loop in the other end of wire.

Swirl Earrings

1. Make a loop.

2. Add beads.

3. Close with loop to add earring wire.

To Make a Bail

Coil 18 gauge Silver wire, pull slightly apart. Cut off 3 loop sections at a time for one or multiple bails. Wind coil onto wire pendant piece at top, push coil together to form bail. Add a decorative touch by turning a loop towards or away from coil. A bail is a very secure connector when adding a slide or pendant to a necklace.

1. Coil wire around dowel.

2. Pull the coil apart.

3. Cut coil in sections of 3 loops.

4. Turn ends in or out for a decorative look.

5. Wind onto pendant.

6. Pinch coil together.

Alternate Bail Directions

Cut 5" of 18 gauge wire. Wrap around a large mandrel or dowel 3-4 times leaving a ½" tail on both sides. Turn loop backwards into tail for decoration. Thread onto pendant. Press coil together to form a bail.

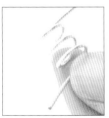 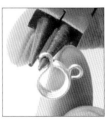

1. Coil wire around a large dowel 3 to 4 times leaving a tail on both ends.

2. Make a ½" loop backwards.

Finished Alternate Bail

Actual Size Bail

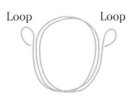

Loop   Loop

'A Little Disc-O' Necklace

Polished discs have a pearlescent sheen that reflects light much like a sequin and looks lovely against the skin.

SIZE: 17"

MATERIALS:
18 gauge Silver wire jump rings (53 large, 4 medium)
• 16 Brown 12mm discs • 7 Turquoise 20mm discs
• Toggle clasp

INSTRUCTIONS:
Load each disc onto a large jump ring. Link formation for necklace is: 11 empty jump rings, Brown, Brown, empty, Turquoise, repeat the bead formation 6 more times, ending with 11 empty jump rings. Add 2 medium jump rings on each end. Attach a toggle clasp.

Aqua Extravagance Choker

Regal in appearance, sparkling in its allure, this shimmering necklace is a must-have addition to any jewelry wardrobe.

SIZE: 14"

MATERIALS:
Silver non-tarnish wire (20 gauge, 18 gauge) • Coil bead • 19 to 23 Aqua crack glass coin 14mm beads • Assorted beads (4 Clear faceted 8mm round, 1 Silver flower spacer, 1 Silver 3.2mm round)

INSTRUCTIONS:
Choker: Cut three 30" strands of Silver wire. Thread all 3 strands through coil bead, place in the middle of the wire length, flatten coil bead. This holds the wires together tightly making it easier to use and becomes the choker center. Slightly bend outside strands left and right. Load Aqua coin bead onto middle strand, take one side strand and bend around bead, cross over middle wire at bead top, loop under middle wire and

pull straight out. Depending on sizing, add 8-11 more beads with same process. Repeat on opposite side. To finish off wire ends, turn an oval loop in each end with middle wire. Wrap with side wires to secure, trim excess.

Choker Dangle: Cut 6" of wire. Make loop wrap in one end, add bead formation, close with loop wrap. Make 3 single bead loop units with Clear beads. Group all 3 and attach to bottom of long dangle with a small jump ring. Attach dangle to choker center with medium jump ring over flattened coil bead. Flatten medium jump ring if necessary to hold in place.

Choker Closure: Make a swirl hook with 4" of 18 gauge Silver wire. Attach to oval loop on one side, hook swirl through other loop for closure.

How to Braid

1. Add bead to the center wire.

2. Bend 1 side strand around bead, loop around middle wire.

3. Bend other side strand around bead, loop around middle wire.

4. Add bead to center wire.

Braiding Diagram

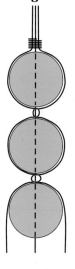

Braiding

For those who love the look and feel of a braid, enjoy an intriguing new twist by braiding around a bead. Every time you change beads you create a unique look.

BASIC WIRE BRAIDING INSTRUCTIONS:

While working with this technique, work flat and bend jewelry piece once complete to fit your wrist or neck.

Cut 3 equal lengths of 20 gauge wire, generally 11" will make a 7" bracelet, 24"-30" for necklace/choker.

You can cut longer wires for a longer bracelet and trim any excess.

Unlike braiding hair, start in the middle of wire to secure wire in place while working.

Holding all 3 wire strands together in the middle of the wire length, add bead to middle strand. Slightly bend the outside strands, take one side strand and bend it around a bead, cross over the middle wire at the bead top, loop it under the middle wire and pull it straight out.

Repeat on remaining side. Add another bead, take one side strand and bend around bead, cross over middle wire at bead top, loop under middle wire and pull straight out.

Turn the piece upside down and repeat the same steps.

Add as many beads as desired.

To finish off wire ends, turn an oval loop in each end with middle wire, wrap with side wires to secure, and trim excess or turn a loop in each wire strand and continue with a swirl.

Amber Allure Earrings

Dripping with sparkle, earrings are too gorgeous to resist. Make a pair this afternoon, wear them tonight.

SIZE: 2"

MATERIALS:
20 gauge non-tarnish Silver wire • 6-8 Amber faceted round 6mm beads • 2 earring wires

INSTRUCTIONS:
Cut 3 equal lengths of wire 4" long. Braid 3 beads per earring. Using middle strand, close top with wrapped loop. Turn loop and swirl in side strands. Add earring wire to top. At bottom of braided section, wrap side strands around middle once, trim. Turn large loop with middle strand. • Make loop bead unit with 1 bead and dangle from bottom of braided section, hooking together by slightly opening loop and closing again.

Amber Allure Bracelet

Adorn your wrist with the allure of amber. This exquisite bracelet has a gorgeous spiral finish.

BRACELET SIZES: 7" TO 7½"

MATERIALS:
20 gauge wire (non-tarnish Silver, Black) • 8-10 Amber faceted round 6mm beads

INSTRUCTIONS:
Using wire worker mandrel or small dowel, tightly coil 2" of Black wire. Pull slightly apart to 2½". Cut three 11" strands of Silver wire. Feed all 3 strands into coil. Holding coil in the middle of strand length, bend side strands to the left and right on both sides of coil. Leave middle strand straight. Follow Basic Wire Braiding instructions. Add 4-5 beads on each side until desired size. • Wrap side wires around middle wire once. Add loop to each strand end and swirl. Middle strand should be longest and swirls will hook together for bracelet closure.

Heart of Gold Bracelet

A heart of gold King Midas would envy, this beautiful bracelet is a real eye catcher.

MATERIALS:
Silver non-tarnish wire (20 gauge, 18 gauge) • 17 Amber faceted round 6mm beads • Sterling Silver Heart Add-A-Bead Pendant • 5 head pins

INSTRUCTIONS:
Cut three 11" strands of wire. Follow Basic Wire Braiding instructions. • If your heart has a place to add beads, load each of 5 beads onto a head pin, thread through to back of heart, turn loop to keep in place. Trim excess head pin.
• Using 18 gauge wire, make one S-hook and one hook following instructions on page 4. Attach S-hook to bracelet loop and heart loop. Attach hook to other side of heart allowing closure by hooking onto other bracelet loop.

Braided Triangular Pottery Beads

Braiding acquires fresh appeal with large triangle pottery beads. Finish this bracelet with a hand-carved shell flower for a beautiful earthy look.

MATERIALS:
20 gauge non-tarnish Silver wire • 6-8 Turquoise triangle pottery beads • Natural Coco Shell 30mm flower bead • Coil bead

INSTRUCTIONS:
Using three 11" strands of Silver wire. Thread all three wire strands through coil bead, place in the middle of the wire length, flatten coil bead. • Follow Braided Wire instructions. Add 2-3 more beads. To finish off wire ends, turn an oval loop in each end with middle wire, wrap with side wires to secure, trim excess.

Flower Clasp: Cut 5" of 20 gauge wire. Thread flower bead onto wire, holding in middle of wire, turn a loop in both ends adding a small swirl. Each hook or side should measure about ¾" when complete. Bend tightly under flower. Slide 1 swirl hook through bracelet loop. Open and close bracelet with swirl hook on under side of flower.

Swirl Finish with Flower Clasp: Cut two 2" lengths of 18 gauge wire. Turn a loop and loose swirl in each piece, leaving a ½" tail. Turn a loop in tail to hook onto bracelet loops. Slide flower clasp into swirls to close bracelet.

Back Detail

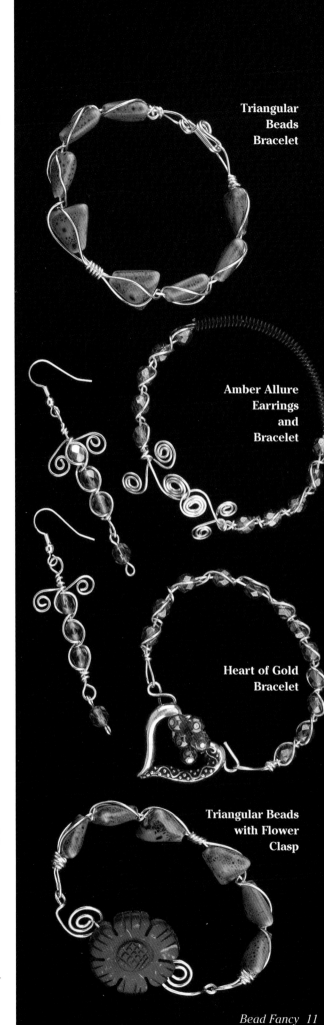

Triangular Beads Bracelet

Amber Allure Earrings and Bracelet

Heart of Gold Bracelet

Triangular Beads with Flower Clasp

Brown Tranquility Bracelet

Capture natural beauty with amber colored stone and turquoise beads - an easy yet eye-catching bracelet.

SIZE: 8"

MATERIALS:
20 gauge non-tarnish Silver wire • Amber matte Silver oval beads (one 20mm, two 12mm) • 8 Turquoise discs • Toggle clasp

INSTRUCTIONS:

Turquoise loop bead units: 4 single bead units, 2 double bead units. Set aside. • **Amber loop bead units**: Make loop bead units with amber beads. Cut two 4" wires, feed one through large Amber bead unit leaving more wire on one side. Turn a loop and large loose swirl in one side, bend down into place on top of bead, carefully following the lines of the bead. Pull remaining wire taut, turn a loop in wire and make a small swirl, bend down into place on top of bead opposite larger swirl. Wire swirls should fit snugly. If needed, slightly press wires down with flat-nose or nylon jaw pliers. • Because the size of the large bead may cause it to turn when worn, apply wrapping embellishment to both sides. Cut two 2" wires, feed one through each small Amber bead unit leaving more wire on one side than the other. Add loop to both sides & swirl, bending swirls in place on top of bead.

Bracelet Formation: Link bead units together through loops by slightly opening loop, threading bead unit, close loop. Formation is left to right: single Turquoise, small Amber bead, double Turquoise, single Turquoise, large Amber bead, single Turquoise, double Turquoise, small Amber bead, single Turquoise. Add medium jump rings to each side, attach toggle clasp.

Making a Wrapped Loop Bead

1. Make bead loop unit.

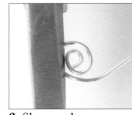

2. Shape a loose swirl.

3. Add a bead.

4. Bend the swirl down around bead.

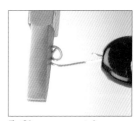

5. Shape a swirl on the other end of wire.

Burst Earrings

Give your earring collection a burst of flair with these pretty dangles.

SIZE: 2¼"

MATERIALS:
20 gauge non-tarnish Silver wire • 10 Teal E-beads • 6 Copper spacer beads • 2 Turquoise discs • 2 small jump rings • 2 earring wires

INSTRUCTIONS:

Burst: Make 6 bead wrap units. See page 4. Use a variety of bead combinations to create interest. Sizes should range from ¾" to 1" when complete. • Cut two 5" pieces of wire. Load bead wrap units onto each wire through looped end to dangle. Take ends of wire between thumb and index finger and bend upwards and across to form a ½" teardrop shaped burst. Cut 2"-3" of wire to wrap the intersection 3-4 times to hold teardrop shape leaving a 1" tail on either side of top. Trim if necessary. Turn a loop in both sides and make a tight swirl, pull and bend swirls outward in a curved over fashion.
Earrings: Make a hinge with 1½" of wire for each earring. See instructions below. Add 2 small linked jump rings and earring wire for final touches.

The Burst of Hope Pendant

Make a burst look spectacular. Beaded dangles adorn the Burst of Hope with creativity, character and movement.

SIZE: 17" necklace, 3" long pendant

MATERIALS:
Silver non-tarnish wire (18 gauge, 20 gauge) • 22-25 Teal E beads, set 2-4 aside • 26 Copper spacer beads, set 10 aside • 11 Turquoise discs • 17" Brown cotton cord • 2 coil ends • 2" length of chain • Lobster claw clasp

INSTRUCTIONS:

Burst: Using 20 gauge wire, make 11 bead wrap units. See page 4. Use a variety of bead combinations to create interest. Sizes should range from 1¼" to 2" when complete. • Cut 9" of 18 gauge wire. Load bead wrap units onto straight wire through looped end with 1 Copper spacer between each bead unit. Add 1 Teal bead to beginning and end of bead units. Once wire is loaded with beads, take ends of wire between thumb and index finger and bend upwards and across to form burst or large teardrop shape. Cut 3" to 4" of 20 gauge wire. Wrap burst top intersection 5-7 times to hold it together leaving a 2" tail on either side of top. Trim to match if necessary. Turn a loop in both sides and make a tight swirl, pull and bend swirls outward in a curved over fashion.
Hinge: Cut 2" of 18 gauge wire. Bend into a "U" over a large dowel or wire worker mandrel. Add 2-4 Teal beads holding in a "U" position. Turn a large loop in both ends of "U". Open loops slightly and attach to top of burst. Close loops.
Necklace: Cut five 16" pieces of Brown cotton cord. Group together adding coil ends to both ends of cord. Add 2" of chain to one side and a lobster claw clasp to other side for closure.

Making a Burst for the Necklace and Earrings

1. Bend wire into teardrop. Add beads.

2. Wrap intersection tightly.

3. Shape swirls in each end.

4. Shape wire over a dowel to form a "U" for hinge.

5. Form loops on each end.

6. Hook loops around the top of the burst.

Around the World Pendant Slide

This stunning bead was blown to include a pendant connection or loop at the top.

SIZE: 2½"

MATERIALS:
18 gauge non-tarnish Silver wire • 30mm Blue/Green round glass pendant bead

INSTRUCTIONS:
Using 11" of wire, make a 1¼" loop in the middle of wire for top of pendant. Feed wire legs through bead loop, crossing them over to opposite side of bead. From the right, following the curves of the bead edge, bend the wire down and around clockwise over to left side of bead stopping at 7:00 position. Repeat from the left side, following the curves of the bead edge. Bring the wire down and around counter clockwise, stopping to twist with other wire at the 7:00 position. This will hold the first wire in place. • Turn a loop and loose swirl into first wire, bending it over top of bead. Continue on with second wire, running it across and behind bead over to the 2:00 position. Bend wire forward to front of bead, add a loop and loose swirl, bending it in place over the top of the bead. The swirls act like little brackets, encasing the bead in wire. Add a bail to top loop. See instructions on page 9.

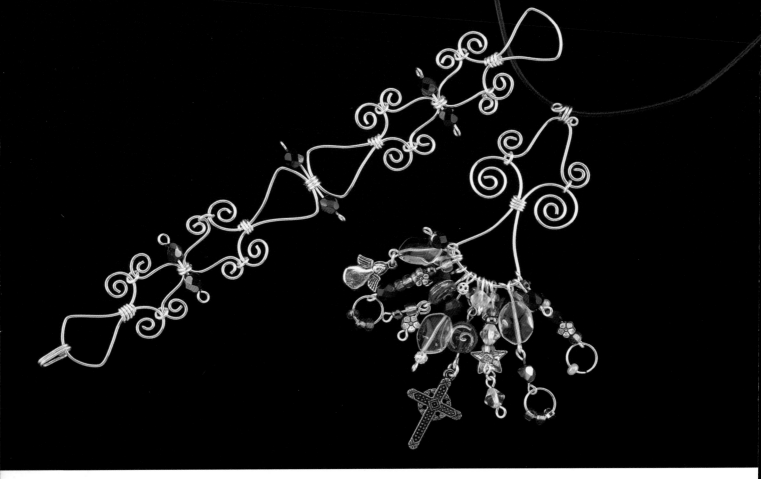

Making the Necklace Pendant

1. Use your thumb and index finger to curve the wire.

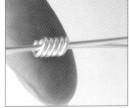

2. Thread a coil wire bead over the join of the pendant.

3. Crimp with pliers.

4. Turn a loop.

5. Make a loose swirl with ends of wire.

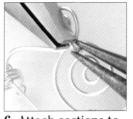

6. Attach sections together with jump rings.

'Charms of Life' Necklace Pendant

Wire flows, bends, shapes and holds intriguing patterns. Use this basic pattern to design unique jewelry pieces.

SIZE: 21" necklace, 4" pendant

MATERIALS:

Silver non-tarnish wire (18 gauge, 20 gauge) • Assorted bead mix (Pink, Black, Clear, Pink twist, Pink bicone, Smoky coin beads, Black faceted beads, 8mm beads) • Charms (Angel, Star, Cross) • Silver spacer beads (Flowers, 4mm balls, Diamonds) • 20" Black leather cord • Coil ends • Jump rings (Large, Small) • Coil wire beads

INSTRUCTIONS:

Dangles: Using 20 gauge wire, make 16 loop bead units. See page 6. Use a variety of bead combinations in sizes from $\frac{1}{2}$" to $1\frac{1}{4}$". Dangle charms from loop bead units with small jump rings. Also add large jump rings with beads on them to the ends of several loop bead units.

Fleur-de-lis: Cut $11\frac{1}{2}$" of 18 gauge wire. From ends of wire, measure in 5" towards center. Using round-nose pliers, bend a right angle. Repeat on other side. The middle section is now 1"-$1\frac{1}{2}$" wide. Using your fingers, slightly curve up like a slight smile. Holding the wire piece with middle section to the top and ends to the bottom, run your thumb down each wire side adding a little pressure to concave and curve each wire side. Slide coil wire bead onto wire ends stopping where wires come together to form a triangle. Triangle should be about $1\frac{1}{4}$". Using flat-nose or nylon jaw pliers, slowly flatten coil bead to hold wire formation in place. Make sure remaining arms are the same length, about $2\frac{1}{2}$". Trim if needed. Bend out wire arms by running your thumb down the wire length and gently pulling, turn loop in each end, swirl loosely on both sides.

Decorative Hinge: Cut 4" of 18 gauge wire. Bend into a "U" over a large dowel or wire worker mandrel. Turn a loop in each end and swirl loosely. Attach hinge to top of Fleur de lis with 2 small jump rings. • Add decorative bail to top of hinge. See page 9.

Add Charms: Slightly open top of loop bead units and load onto Fleur-de-lis charm pendant in a random formation intermixing long and short bead units. Close loops again.

Necklace: Cut 20" of Black leather cord. Add coil end to both sides. Add a medium jump ring to both sides and a hook clasp to one side for closure.

Making the Bracelet Hook

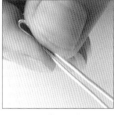

1. Bend 2" - 3" of wire in half.

2. Bend loops into each end.

3. Bend loop into folded end.

4. Bend middle to form a hook for the bracelet closure.

Ironwork Bracelet

With or without the added sparkle of beads, Ironwork is elegant to behold and distinctive to wear.

SIZE: 7½"

MATERIALS:
Silver non-tarnish wire (18 gauge, 20 gauge) • 6 Black faceted round 8mm beads • Small jump rings • Coil wire beads

INSTRUCTIONS:
Links: Following instructions for the Charms of Life necklace, make 4 fleur-de-lis with 5" of 18 gauge wire for each link. Bend right angle at 2" on both sides leaving a 1" center section. Continue as directed. • Make 4 decorative hinges with 3" of 18 gauge wire for each link.
Bracelet: Lay bracelet links on a flat surface. Assemble left to right: Fleur, hinge, hinge, fleur, fleur, hinge, hinge, fleur. Link these pieces together with small jump rings at swirls or middles depending where they touch. Swirls use 1 jump ring on each side, middles use 2 jump rings and center of bracelet middle uses 3 jump rings.
Add beads: The middle bead section needs to be a little longer than the side bead sections to lie nicely on wrist. • Cut three 2" lengths from 18 gauge wire. Turn a loop in one end, load Black bead, slide through small jump rings that meet in the middle, load another Black bead, turn a loop to close, trim excess wire as needed. Repeat twice.
Hook: Make hook following instructions above. Add hook directly to 1 side of bracelet to close.

Bead Wrapping

Bead wrapping is an excellent way to showcase fabulous beads. This is not a traditional bead wrapping approach where you encase a round bead in wire and swirls. In this technique, the bead shape, curve, texture, and color dictates the design.

Bead wrapping can turn a plain bead into a spectacular and dramatic pendant piece.

BASIC WIRE WRAPPING INSTRUCTIONS:
Use 18 or 20 gauge wire when wrapping a bead, matching smaller beads with thinner wire for flexibility. Begin with more wire than you think you will need. It is always easier to trim but difficult to add extra wire to your piece when wrapping. Finish ends with a decorative loop or swirl so there are no raw ends. When wrapping, gauge your wire design so the beauty of your bead is showcased.

Lotus Flower Pendants

Lovely as a Lotus blossom, the silver inside the beads cause this simple pendant to shimmer in the light.

SIZE: 5½" before bending

MATERIALS:
20 gauge non-tarnish Silver wire • 20 gauge Black wire • 2 Blue or Amber matte Silver 20mm oval beads

INSTRUCTIONS:
Using wire worker small mandrel or dowel, coil Black wire tightly to make a 3" coil. Pull slightly apart to 3½". Cut two 9" Silver wires. Feed both wire strands through coil leaving 3"- 4" on either side of coil. • Make bail following instructions on page 9. Thread bail onto Black coil. • Add bead to one side, separate wire strands, turn a loop and loose swirl in both strands. Pull wire taut and repeat on opposite side. • Bend coil into a large loop with one side being a little longer than the other.

Door Knocker
Pendant and Earrings

Stylish and modern, the clean lines of the tube beads complement the lime green rounds for an accessory in today's most popular colors.

SIZE: 2" pendant, 1½" earrings

MATERIALS:
18 gauge non-tarnish Silver wire • 16 Lime Green round 4mm beads • 3 Aqua faceted tube beads • 2 ear wires

INSTRUCTIONS:
Pendant: Cut 6" wire. Turn a loop in one end and make a medium swirl. Load 4 Lime beads, 1 Aqua bead and 4 Lime beads. Turn a loop in opposite end of wire and make another medium swirl, matching size of first. At this point, the piece should be straight with swirls on both ends going the same direction with beads in the middle with a little extra wire between beads and swirls. Holding the swirled ends between thumb and index finger, bend slowly upwards to create a large loop looking similar to a door knocker or a saddle stirrup. Swirls should almost meet at top.

Hinge Dangle: Cut a 2½" wire. Bend into a "U" over large dowel or wire worker mandrel. Turn a large loop in both ends of "U". Open loops up slightly and feed through swirls on each side of pendant piece. Close loops. • See Bail instructions on page 9. Add bail to top of pendant.

Earrings: Cut two 3" wires. Make earring pieces following pendant instructions using 2 lime beads, 1 Aqua bead, and 2 lime beads for each. • Make hinge dangle with above instructions using two 2" pieces of wire. Connect earrings pieces together through swirl centers. Add earring wires to top of hinge.

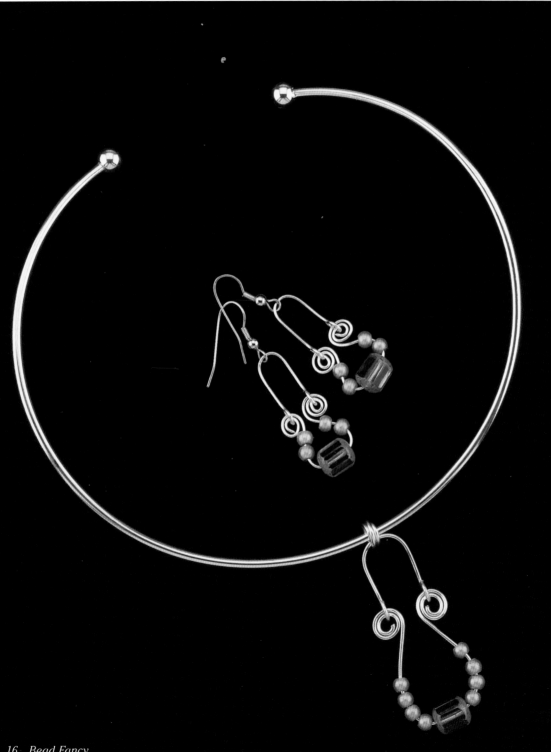

Making the Center Burst

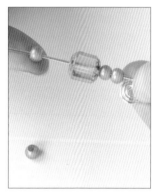

1. Shape swirl. Add beads.

2. Shape swirl to close.

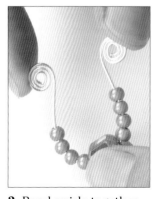

3. Bend swirls together.

Making the Pendant Slide for the Necklace

1. Coil 3 loops around dowel.

2. Squeeze the wire coils together.

Begin with 5" of wire. Wrap around a dowel 3-4 times leaving a ½" tail on both sides. Make loops in tails for decoration.

Actual Size Bail Slide

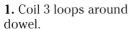

Making the Top Hinge for the Earrings

1. Shape a "U" around a wooden dowel.

2. Form a loop in each end.

Actual Size Center Burst and Earring Shapes

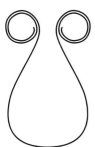

Encasing Love Pendant

Wrapped beads can be bold and graphic or delicately feminine. Encasing Love captures the spirit of the romantic heart.

SIZE: 24" necklace
　　　　3" long pendant

MATERIALS:
Silver non-tarnish wire (20 gauge, 26 gauge) • 25 x 20mm Pink Silver foiled glass heart bead • Assorted bead mix (Clear, Silver, Pink, Green, Silver spacers) • 23" Brown organza ribbon ⅞" wide • Crimp ends • Medium jump rings

INSTRUCTIONS:
Encase heart: Use the bead hole to hold the wire in place to start. Using a 14" piece of 20 gauge wire, make a ¾" loop in the middle of the wire for top of pendant. Feed wire legs down through bead hole and out bottom. Separate wire ends, bending each up the side of the glass heart following the heart curves, bending each side over the heart humps, crossing in the middle at the top. Bring wires down over middle of heart to the bottom and back up crossing again at top of heart. Bend remaining wire over top middle of heart to other side, bending in place. Add a loop to each end and trim excess if needed.

Dangles: Using 6" of 26 gauge wire, bend in half leaving a small loop in middle. Feed wire ends through bottom of bead hole to top, wrap loose ends around base of large loop to secure in place. Trim excess wire. • Make 5-8 small loop bead units varying in size from ¾" to 1" to dangle from heart bottom. Group together with medium jump ring. Attach to bottom of heart loop with a small jump ring. Add a bail to top loop. See bail instructions on page 9 and at left.

Necklace: Add crimp ends, medium jump rings and clasp to ends of organza ribbon.

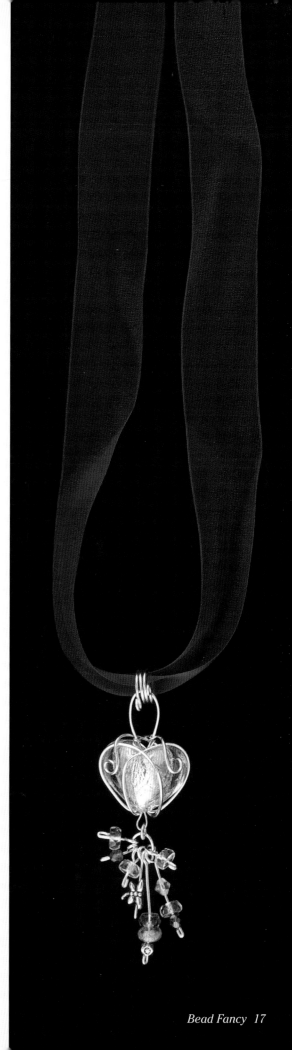

Andrea Gibson

I love making things with my hands and sharing my creativity with others. It is my goal to bring you beautiful projects that you can learn from, that you will love making, and that will inspire you to creatively apply what you have learned.

For me, working with wire truly inspires uncountable crafty ideas. I've designed projects and taught crafters to become confident when using wire for many applications. My newest love for wire is in designing and making jewelry pieces. I'm bringing to you in this book easy techniques and tricks to make your wire jewelry pieces quick, easy, beautiful and best of all, enviable.

You will also find my work in PaperCrafts, Rubber Stamper, Scrapbook Etc., Paperkuts, Scrapbook Retailer, and books by Design Originals.

You can contact me at andreagibson@earthlink.net for classes and questions.

Suppliers - Most craft and variety stores carry an excellent assortment of supplies. If you need something special, ask your local store to contact the following companies:

WIRE, WIRE WORKER SYSTEM
   Artistic Wire

BEADS
   The Beadery
   Blue Moon Beads
   Blumenthal Lansing Company
   Cousin Corporation of America
   Crafts, Etc.
   Halcraft USA

MANY THANKS to my friends for their cheerful help and wonderful ideas!

Kathy McMillan • Patty Williams
Donna Kinsey • Diana McMillan
David & Donna Thomason

Making the Pink Dangles for Earrings

1. Shape a swirl at the end of the wire.

2. Add beads to the wire.

3. Make a loop at the top of the wire.

4. Join the loops with a jump ring.

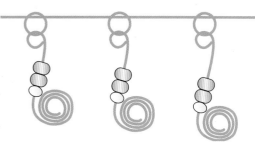

Pink Dangle Earrings

SIZE: 1½"
MATERIALS:
20 gauge non-tarnish Silver wire • 2 medium jump rings • 12 Pink beads • 6 Clear beads
INSTRUCTIONS:
Make 6 single swirls adding 1 clear and 2 Pink beads to each. Vary the length of each swirl, from ¾" - 1". Link swirl dangles together with a jump ring through top loop. Add earring wire to jump ring.

Blue and Green Harmony Jewelry Set

Try this dramatic set for your jewelry collection. The swirl beads look amazing when loaded onto the necklace. Randomly swirling in different directions produces a beautiful freeform fashion.

SIZE: 19" necklace, 9" bracelet, 1½" earrings
MATERIALS:
Silver non-tarnish wire (18 gauge, 20 gauge) • 29 Peridot faceted tube beads • 29 Amethyst faceted tube beads • Jump rings for earrings (2 large, 2 small)
INSTRUCTIONS:
"S" Swirls: Make 25 "S" swirls referring to "S" swirl directions (12 Peridot and 13 Amethyst). Load faceted tube bead before starting second loop.
Necklace: Using 18 gauge wire, cut a 20" piece and harden it by pulling it through nylon jaw pliers a few times to smooth out any tiny ripples. Bend a hook closure in one end of wire. Load necklace wire with S swirls through faceted bead alternating colors. Bend an eye closure into end of necklace wire.
Bracelet: Make 26 "S" swirls, 13 Peridot and 14 Amethyst. Construct as necklace using 12" of 18 gauge wire.
Earrings: For each earring, make 2 Peridot and 1 Amethyst swirl. Link "S"swirls together with a large jump ring through the center of a swirl. Attach to earring wire with 2 small linked jump rings. If desired, unwind the Amethyst swirl a bit to add extra length and dimension to earring.

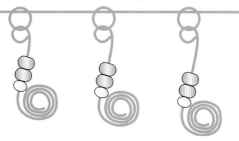